Insight for Living

Devotional prayer focus for 3 day, 21 day and 40 day fast – insightful words to help you tap into the heart of God.

By
Dr. Coraleen F. Braxton

Insight for Living
Leading Lady Publications
A Division of Anointed Word Media Group
1-800-597-9428
P.O. Box 35, Worton, MD 21678
www.publishyourchristianbook.com
Cover Design by: Tamika Johnson-Hall
ISBN-10: 0-9802468-1-4
ISBN-13: 978-0-9802468-1-0
Copyright © 2007 by Dr. Coraleen F. Braxton

Printed in the United States of America

To order additional copies please contact:
Anointed Word Media Group
1-800-597-9428
info@publishyourchristianbook.com
www.anointedwordbookstore.net

All scriptures are taken from the King James Version unless otherwise stated. © 2007

Dedication

To all intercessors, as you keep watch with the Lord may this book inspire you to keep the flame burning. You are chosen to impact the atmosphere with the presence of God. God is ready to move in the earth and He desires to do it through you.

Acknowledgements

I wish to thank Dr. Corinthia Boone-Ridgley for believing in me and challenging me to write these devotions which were birthed out of weekly emails to encourage "Together In Ministry's" pastors and intercessors. You are a great inspiration to me and the Body of Christ.

I am gratefully indebted to the Father, Son, and Holy Spirit for all the times well spent in Your presence. It is always a joy to be with You. I would not have it any other way. My desire is to always bless You in whatever I say or do. To God be the glory!

FOREWARD

These daily devotions, if you will read, meditate and let the Spirit of God speak to your spirit, will lift you up each day- not just to guide you in your daily activity but to help you sense the presence of the Lord throughout the day.

Carefully consider each scripture reference in these devotions. Author Coraleen Braxton has skillfully matched each day's meditations with these scriptures. These devotions alert us to realize that new wine (new revelations, a new season, new anointing) must be put into new bottles that both may be preserved.

Coraleen exhorts us to arise as the corporate Body of Christ, to rise above our individuality. When God gives someone a vision, the entire Body of Christ should come together and support what God desires to do through His people.

God has designed armor for every believer, young and old, married or single; never leave home without it. Could we say, never start the day without your morning devotion.

The world waits for the manifestation of the Sons of God; the world needs us. God intends for us to take a part in His plan to restore all humanity. When we look upon obeying as a right rather than a task, as true sons of God, we can expect blessings.

Think about the peace of God. Yet on our part it will take concentrated effort to change and change comes only at a price. That price includes dethroning the flesh.

In these devotions, you will find examples from both the Old and New Testaments along with practical applications to our daily lives as well as personal experiences of Coraleen.

Richard W. Rundell
Author, Evangelist

Day 1

Surprise Visitation

Luke 1:78
Because of the tender mercy of our God, with which the Sunrise from on high <u>shall visit us</u>...

We cannot find one person in this world who does not enjoy pleasant surprises; especially a surprise visit from a friend. We remember Elizabeth when Mary surprised her with an unexpected visit. The life inside of Elizabeth leaped with joy so that she was provoked to bless and honor Mary.

As we pray and watch with the Lord, His presence will began to inhabit our surroundings, because this is His desire. Dr. Chuck Pierce ascribes to five topics to help us understand the Lord's visitation: (1) <u>There is a time of visitation</u>. We realize two Greek words for *"time"* – <u>*chronos*</u> and *kairos*. Chronos refers to chronological time -- days, weeks, months and years. Kairos refers to an appointed time or an opportune time. God sets aside kairos time for visitation (Luke 19:43-44). (2) <u>During times of visitation miraculous blessings come</u>. When Jesus moved among the people tremendous blessings occurred…the blind received their sight, the deaf heard, the lame walked, the dead were raised up, sins were forgiven and so on. We should not expect anything less but should cry out for His blessing when He comes (Mk 10:46-52). (3) <u>Faithfulness and consistency produce surprise visitation</u>. When we are found trustworthy in the service of the Lord, those barren places in our lives become a catalyst for visitation – when we least expect to hear from Him (Luke 1:13-15). (4) <u>Visitation secures our inheritance</u>. Job 10:12, "Thou hast granted me life and favour, and thy <u>visitation</u> hath preserved my spirit." The Hebrew word for preserve is *shamar* which means to guard, keep safe, protect, watch over or care for. As God manifests Himself through visitation, He is preserving His purposes for our lives, and securing our inheritance. (5) <u>Visitation produces glory</u>! When the true manifest presence of God visits us as humans, it cannot be done without His glory radiating from that presence (Read Exodus 33: 18, 22; 40:34-35).

Day 2

Living in the *Shekianh* Presence of God

Leviticus 9:6
And Moses said, "This is the thing which the LORD has commanded you to do, that the glory of the LORD may appear to you."

Some interesting insight I believe God wants to bring to our level of understanding. Many may already know this...but for those unaware, and to those that need reminding, such as myself, we as people of God, have the power and authority to continually live in the shekinah presence of God.

I believe if we understand the concept that God gave Moses on how to keep the tabernacle as a place where the shekinah could dwell, it will help us to continually live in His shekinah glory. (1) The Altar of Burning Offering (see Lev. 6:9-3). Daily, we should offer our lives up to God as an act of worship. (2) The Table of Showbread (see Lev. 24). God desires continual thanksgiving for His goodness and provision. (3) The Golden Lampstand (see Lev. 24). This symbolized the presence of the Holy Spirit. We must continually fellowship with the Holy Spirit. (4)

<u>The Altar of Incense</u> (see Exodus 29:42-46). This is symbolic of the prayers of the saints rising to God. We are commanded to "<u>pray without ceasing</u>".

God says to us, that if we build a living tabernacle of continual prayer, praise and worship, *He will meet us and speak to us, and the place will be sanctified by His glory...then He will dwell among us*.

<u>Just to summarize</u>...two <u>principles to remember</u>: (1) Where there is prayer, praise, and thanksgiving, <u>God's presence will come</u>, and (2) Where there is <u>continual</u> prayer, praise, and thanksgiving, <u>God's presence will dwell</u>.

Day 3

Seek the Lord and Live – The Hour Commands It!

Amos 5:4
For thus saith the LORD unto the house of Israel, Seek ye me, and ye shall live:

God destined America to be a great nation because our forefathers established this nation on Christian principles. Billy Graham said, "America was not just to be a Christian nation but a nation of Christians."

We will discover two Old Testament scriptures which gives credence to Dr. Graham's statement: "And Ruth said ... thy people shall be my people and thy God my God" (Ruth 1:16); secondly, "And Ittai answered the king, and said, as the Lord lives ...even there also will thy servant be" (2 Samuel 15:21).

The hour commands that we choose whom to serve and pledge allegiance. It is not popular in this day-and-time to stand for justice and righteousness or maintain integrity. Consequently, if we walk in this manner we find the road narrow.

We are living in a day that Amos prophetically spoke about:

God urges America to Return to Him: (1) He has given us empty stomachs and lack of bread (Amos 4:6); (2) Natural disasters have affected this nation (v. 7); and (3) Our crops and vineyard have not fully developed because of the global weather patterns (v. 9) yet, we have not returned to the Lord! God calls for America to lament in the streets, square, and vineyards and repent because judgment is inevitable.

Our nation is defined by our court system – It is proven in scriptures that there is no fear of God anymore: (1) We have turned justice into bitterness and cast righteousness to the ground (Amos 5:7); (2) We hate those who reprove in court and despise anyone who tells the truth (v. 10); and (3) We oppress the righteous and take bribes and deprive the poor of justice (v. 12).

But, we discover a reoccurring theme in Amos chapter 5, God says, (1) "Seek Me and live" (v. 5); (2) "Seek the Lord and live" (v. 6); (3) "Seek Good, not evil that you may live" (v. 14); and (4) "Hate evil, love Good; maintain justice in the courts" (v. 15).

Our religious assemblies have become a stench in the nostril of God because we do not stand up for holiness and truth. We fear that our numbers will drop (v. 21).

But God says, "Let justice roll like a river, righteousness like a never-failing stream" (v. 24). As plants and animals grow in the midst of water, America will prosper in the midst of justice and righteousness. We must seek the Lord– the hour commands it!

Day 4

It is *Due* Time for Corporate Intercession in America!

Joel 2:13-14
… "And <u>rend your heart</u>, and not your garments, <u>and turn unto the Lord your God</u>: for <u>He</u> is <u>gracious</u> and <u>merciful, slow to anger, and of great kindness</u>, <u>and repent</u> Him of the evil. <u>Who knows if He</u> will return and repent, and <u>leave a blessing behind Him</u>; even a meat offering and a drink offering unto the <u>Lord your God</u>?"

America must <u>arise as a corporate Body and cry out with intercession</u>! The time has now come. The Bible records many examples where <u>God responded to intercession</u>:
(1) Abraham pleaded for Sodom – Genesis 18:16-35 reveals that Abraham went to God on six accounts with intercession. (2) In 1 Samuel 7:3-6, Samuel <u>interceded</u> for the Israelites and the Lord <u>subdued their enemy</u> (Philistines) in battle. (3) Amos, in chapter 7:2, 5 cried out to the Lord to <u>avert judgment</u> on Jacob <u>and the Lord relented</u>. And (4) <u>Jesus' intercession</u> will <u>save all</u> who <u>come</u> to God (Heb. 7:23-25).

What about America's <u>unfaithfulness,</u> <u>idolatry</u> and <u>rejection of God</u>! <u>Where are we</u>??? The Bible also records in Jeremiah numerous occasions when God <u>rejected intercession</u>: (1) Jeremiah 7:16, "Therefore <u>pray not</u> thou for this people…for <u>I will not hear thee</u>." (2) Jeremiah 11:14, "Therefore <u>pray not</u> thou for this people…for <u>I will not hear them</u> in the time that they cry unto me for their trouble." And (3) Jeremiah 14:11, "Then said <u>the Lord</u> unto me, <u>Pray not for this people</u> for their good."

Throughout the Old Testament, <u>Israel's</u> <u>sins had filled God's cup of wrath</u> and once again God was ready to pour it out upon them. <u>No man could bring a charge against the priest</u> <u>or accuse one another</u> - all had <u>rejected God</u> <u>and His ways</u>. Consequently, God's mercy had run out and now they would reap for their sins, <u>yet, Jesus</u> has <u>provided</u> a <u>better covenant</u>: "Wherefore <u>He</u> is able also to <u>save them</u> to the uttermost that <u>come unto</u> <u>God</u> by Him, seeing <u>He ever lives</u> to make <u>intercession for them</u>" (Hebrews 7:25). So let us make a concerted effort to assemble together and intercede on behalf of America. God waits for us!

Day 5

Overcoming to Become!

Romans 8:19
For the earnest expectation of the creature waiteth for the manifestation of the sons of God.

To become is to come to be what God has designed for us before the beginning of the world. In Jeremiah 1:5, God declares that before we were formed in the womb, He knew and consecrated us to do His purposes. He has nothing but good thoughts towards us that we might have a wonderful future.

Jeremiah 29:11
"For I know the thoughts that I think toward you," saith the LORD, "thoughts of peace, and not of evil, to give you an expected end. "

We overcome in two ways: First when we accept Jesus in our life for what He has done for us on the cross. We are transformed out of darkness into His marvelous light. Second, we overcome in our daily Christian walk, a continual process. The more we obey Christ, the more we are transformed into Christ-likeness. We became a son; now it's time to mature as a son of God.

We tend to look at obeying as a task rather than a right. A task is imposed upon us as a labor, but a right is a privilege or a lawful claim to something. Therefore, when we obey we have the right to obey and <u>expect blessings of a son</u>; which a slave does not receive.

One of the major blessings is that we do not subject ourselves to the law, because the law is for law-breakers. But those who obey the law of the Spirit, God rewards with <u>total freedom</u>! We don't have to constantly look over our shoulders wondering if God will apprehend us for our disobedience.

When we obey we will not have to live in unforgiveness, regret or shame for our conduct. In fact <u>our obedience to Christ stands as our greatest accomplishment in life</u>. Man thinks that material wealth, degrees, and status are his greatest accomplishments, but God determines success entirely different from man.

Remember, an overcoming life will require <u>total absolute abandonment</u> to the will of the Father, because the hour <u>commands it</u>! To become a mature son as well as a <u>son of God</u> has always been the Father's original intent for us, and the <u>earth groans</u> for that <u>appointed time</u>. So, let's declare, "Thy kingdom come Thy will be done...<u>in me to become</u>!

Day 6
The Lord…A Mighty Warrior

Isaiah 42:12-14
Let them give glory unto the LORD, and declare his praise in the islands. The LORD shall go forth as a mighty man, he shall stir up jealousy like a man of war: he shall cry, yea, roar; he shall prevail against his enemies. I have long time holden my peace; I have been still, *and* refrained myself: *now* will I cry like a travailing woman; I will destroy and devour at once.

God stands ready to <u>march out like a mighty man, like a warrior</u> to stir up His zeal and raise the battle cry (v. 13). As long as we have an adversary, spiritual warfare won't go away; <u>we must learn to fight</u>!

As long as <u>we keep God in His proper place as Commander in Chief</u> we will triumph over <u>His enemies</u>. He will make darkness into light and <u>lead His people by ways they have never known before</u> (v. 16). This text suggests that <u>God desires to lead us</u>, so it is time to put <u>Him in the driver's seat</u>!

Dr. Corinthia Boone says, "America's <u>biblical</u> and <u>spiritual</u> foundation is <u>under</u>

attack. Therefore, God has brought the root of the attacks to the forefront." The enemy now deploys three spiritual destructive forces: (1) Jihadism – The Muslims' holy war, (2) Moral relativism, and (3) Humanism.

However, Christians must keep their focus on the kingdom of God, because demonic forces, by design, distract us from the call of God, which is: (1) To keep our attention on a clear presentation of Christ; (2) Train up the next generation in Christology; (3) Deter the destructive forces of sin; and (4) The Church must return to prayer. This is not negotiable!

Finally, the prevalent mind set in American promotes individualism instead of Christ consciousness which causes division in the Body of Christ.

But God, by His grace and mercy… the Church can change that and reject this present world view and begin again to pray and imitate a biblical world view which values one another.

Therefore, let us re-commit to watch and pray - Press in - This is not the hour to slack up! As we trust in our God we can declare, **"Blessed *be* the LORD my strength,** which teacheth my hands to war, *and* my fingers to fight" (Psalm 144:1).

Day 7
We Are Entering New Territory

Joshua 3:4
Yet there shall be a space between you and it, about two thousand cubits by measure: come not near unto it that ye may know the way by which ye must go: <u>for ye have not passed this *way* heretofore</u>.

We declare it imperative in this hour that we<u> watch and pray</u>. We must not drop our guard or forfeit our possession.

We now enter into <u>new territory</u> which <u>the Lord directs</u>. The question is: will we <u>trust and obey</u> Him to experience the blessings that He has <u>long prepared</u> for us?

We have heard over and again that God <u>blesses us to be a blessing</u>. Yet sometimes we resist to enter into the joy of the Lord because of the major risk involved; <u>Total Abandonment</u>! We know human nature tempts us to take the path of least resistance.

Total Abandonment has a whole lot to do with <u>absolute and irrevocable surrender</u> of our will to the Holy Spirit. "<u>Not my</u> will Lord...but <u>Your will</u> be done in <u>my life</u>!"

How often do we say those words, or pray that statement but when God comes to collect on the <u>deal</u>, we make an excuse and said "<u>No deal!</u>"

The Bible says that everyone is without an <u>excuse;</u> as a matter of fact <u>excuses are tools of the incompetent.</u>

We don't have to make up excuses anymore because <u>we</u> have an <u>Almighty God</u> who is <u>trustworthy and faithful</u>; He <u>does not lie</u> and when <u>we have faith in God</u>, He will make good on what He has promised.

God is <u>able</u> and <u>wants</u> to take us into <u>new territory</u>. It is time for the <u>history makers</u> to <u>come forth</u> and <u>change</u> the world for the <u>sake of the Kingdom</u>. It is <u>imperative</u>. <u>Let's</u> do this <u>together</u>, we are <u>well able!</u>

It is time to <u>step out</u>, <u>dream big</u>, <u>pray bigger prayers,</u> <u>let go</u> and <u>trust God!</u>

Day 8
Declare to the Next Generation

Psalm 71:17-18

O God, thou hast <u>taught</u> me from <u>my youth</u>: and hitherto have I declared thy wondrous works. Now also when I am old and greyheaded, O God, forsake me not; until I have shewed thy strength unto <u>*this* generation</u>, *and* thy power to <u>every one *that* is to come</u>.

The time has come for the older generation to pour into the next generation. We have been given a wonderful opportunity to carry the gospel – <u>the Living Word</u> to a dying world. We must keep this charge so that we will glorify God in <u>our lives</u> and show Himself strong to the <u>nations</u>.

Genesis 18:19 declares that God chose Abraham "so that he will direct <u>his children and his household</u> after him to keep the ways of the Lord by doing what is <u>right and just</u>…"

God is <u>ready</u> to manifest the fulfillment of <u>His promise to Abraham</u> and to his descendents. We, his descendents, toil as co-laborers in the <u>work of the Lord</u> therefore we must work while it is day and take important steps: (1) We must introduce our seed to the ways of the Lord at an early age so when they get old they will not depart from it. (2) We must declare the deeds of Almighty God, whom we serve to the next generation. (3) We must teach our seed to pray to the Father in Jesus' name. And (4) we must teach them to seek Him in all of their ways and to not lean to their own understanding. These steps are basic yet somehow we have fallen short of accomplishing this task. When we look at our world today it may seem that all hope is lost. But where sin abounds, grace abounds much more. Thank God!

Even if we get a late start, it is never too late to start! So let us begin with prayer and fasting, seeking the Lord for strategies on how to accomplish the work He has given us, and then follow-through to completion. Jesus said that He had glorified the Father because He had finished the work that the Father entrusted to Him.

Remember, when we trust the Holy Spirit to work through us it's not that hard!

Day 9

Not on My Watch

Isaiah 21:6
For thus hath the Lord said unto me, Go, set a watchman, let him declare what he seeth.

Sometime ago on a popular secular talk-show I heard the above term (Not On My Watch) used by a group of people that apparently made an impact in the African American community. Even the ancient African proverb, "it takes a village to raise a child" sounded good. I was also impressed by the work that these groups of activists accomplish to prepare the youth to be productive citizens in society.

This scenario stands as a model of what I believe God wants to do through the Church as a whole. My question is: Why does the Church have to go to the government or to the world for help?

The Church prevails as a powerful force in the earth and where God has given the vision, He has given provision. When God gives a particular man or woman a vision, the entire body should come together and support what God desires to do through His people.

Because of the size of such a vision, it will involve us all.

I believe many of the people that God now uses are Christians, which brings me to another point about the program. I was surprised that in this particular talk show they did not mention prayer and fasting as part of this onslaught against ignorance, but they greatly stressed educating our youth. Just as we can confidently speak about education we should be just as bold and confident to speak of prayer and fasting. We need them both! Pray for our Christian leaders whom God is using that they will not fear man but be bold as a lion (Proverb 28:1).

The world speaks about any and everything and doesn't care about offending the Church, but when we speak about Jesus, they find it offensive and politically incorrect. Well, Jesus is Lord and on my watch!

Let us be careful that we don't confuse movement with progress. However, you cannot have progress without movement. (But in order to keep the progress going, you have to change the heart of a person). Without the presence of God, movement is in vain!

Finally, the Apostle Paul declares in Galatians 4:19, "My little children, of whom I travail in birth again until Christ be formed in you", so let us continue to <u>watch and pray with the Lord</u>. <u>Seek His presence</u> and He will <u>bring forth</u> an <u>eternal change in our youth and in us</u> to present us holy and un-blamable and un-reproveable in His sight (Colossians 1:22).

Day 10

Up-grading Our Prayer Strategy

Luke 5:37-38

And no man putteth new wine into old bottles; else the new wine will burst the bottles, and be spilled, and the bottles shall perish. But new wine must be put into new bottles; and both are preserved.

We now live in a new season when <u>God pours out the new wine</u>. Therefore we must be alert and aware of what God is doing in this hour.

The prayer that we have to bring forth this season is different. What people did in the past will not work because it was directed by the flesh of man. There is a new anointing that inhabits <u>the cluster</u> – the <u>Corporate Anointing</u> …where the <u>power lies</u>.

Dr. Corinthia Boone ascribes, "The <u>vision</u> which God is releasing to His people is that it is time to upgrade our prayer techniques thus: (1) Prayer must now be <u>Spirit led</u> versus <u>agenda driven</u>; (2) Prayer must be <u>worship fed</u> versus of <u>our request</u>; and (3) Prayer must now be <u>corporate prayer</u> versus <u>individual prayer in a group setting</u>."

29

Jesus said that <u>what is His - will be revealed to us by the Holy Spirit</u>. The Spirit knows the Father's heart and how we should pray when we don't know how to pray. He has unlimited resources, therefore when we tap into the power source, <u>things will happen</u>! We will begin to see results from our prayers.

Habakkuk <u>caught the vision</u> of the Lord. He wrote it down so that whoever read it could run with it! Let's start <u>practicing</u> these prayer techniques in our <u>private time with God</u> and then we will <u>continue to engage with the Spirit during our corporate times together</u>. We will generate <u>power in agreement</u> and where brothers and sisters <u>come together in unity</u>, <u>God will command a blessing</u>!

Day 11

Don't Leave Home Without It

Ephes. 6:13-17
Wherefore take unto you the whole armour of God that ye may be able to withstand in the evil day, and having done all, to stand. Stand therefore, having your loins girt about with truth, and having on the breastplate of righteousness; And your feet shod with the preparation of the gospel of peace; Above all, taking the shield of faith, wherewith ye shall be able to quench all the fiery darts of the wicked. And take the helmet of salvation, and the sword of the Spirit, which is the word of God:

I have witnessed too many of God's children get beat up by the enemy at their own expense. We know better but we don't consider it significant to put on our spiritual gear – the armor of God. It is spiritual suicide without it!

When we get up in the morning, we all have a daily routine. We brush our teeth, wash our face and shower, shave, put on make-up, comb our hair, put on the clothes that we decided on the night before, then we add the finishing touches of our favorite cologne or perfume; and out the door we go!

Even on the week-ends or a day of annual leave, we give our appearance at least the bare minimal touches. It would be a disgrace to go to out in public any other way in fear we might see someone we know.

Well, Paul <u>warns us</u> in Ephesians that <u>we have an adversary</u> who sits and devises council to trip us up every waking hour of the day. Nevertheless, we choose to leave home without the <u>protective armor</u> that God has provided for our well-being.

If the U.S. soldiers in Iraq went out on the battle field without their guns, <u>knowing</u> that their enemy was waiting for them, what do you think would happen? The answer is obvious! As a matter of fact the news media would suggest that this was a <u>blatant suicide mission</u>. Many of us would probably agree!

You drive in your car and someone cuts us off, and you let out a few choice words. You travel further down the road you come upon an accident that stops all of the traffic and you are already late for work. You finally arrive at work and the boss is having a bad day, so you become the target of his wrath.

You get a call from your child's school that Johnny or Sue has a fever and needs to go home. So you call your spouse and ask if he can see about the child because you can't leave you job – again! The conversation turns sour because due to a big project, he can't leave either. Now whoever is forced to pick up the sick child – it's the child's fault because <u>you did not put on your armor</u>.

But we see only the tip of the iceberg – the rest follows. The enemy will see to it! He has just leashed his principalities, powers and wicked spirits out against you and he enjoys the show at <u>your expense</u>.

The armor of God - He has designed for <u>every believer</u>, whether married, single, male, female, young or old. But in order to stand strong against the devil's schemes, we must button up that armor.

Let's make it practical! Whenever you put on a piece of clothing, comb your hair, put on your shoes, and the finishing touches, pretend it is a piece of your spiritual armor - that way you will never leave home without it.

Day 12

Fear Not

Acts 14:22
"Strengthening the souls of the disciples, encouraging them to continue in the faith, and saying, 'Through many tribulations we must enter the kingdom of God.'"

Many of us God will grant special assignments that only the big name personalities should have received, yet God has qualified us and therefore releases (us) His remnant into the earth. We may not have the backing of <u>man</u> but we will have the <u>support and authority of God</u>.

Our tribulations will consist of many sufferings, troubles, afflictions, persecutions, anguishes and burdens. Yet <u>our actions and responses must reveal the power of God</u>. "For the kingdom of God is not in word, but in <u>power</u>" (1 Corinthians 4:20).

When we are cursed, we should bless; when we are persecuted, we should endure it and when we are slandered, we should answer kindly (1 Corinthians 4:12-13).

Entering the <u>Kingdom of God means walking in a rule or realm of power</u>. This realm of power the enemy will fight against us through releasing the attacks. However, God will use the tribulations for His glory!

Our tribulations work death in our mortal body, but life works in the many who will receive from us. Also, God will help us to strengthen and encourage the disciples to remain true to the faith.

Fear not! Be encouraged, because we have treasures in jars of clay that need to come forth to show the all-surpassing power of God (2 Corinthians. 4:7).

Day 13

The Church's Glory - Sonship

Romans 8:19-22

For the anxious longing of the creation waits eagerly for the revealing of the sons of God. For the creation was subjected to futility, not of its own will, but because of Him who subjected it, in hope that <u>the creation itself also will be set free from its slavery to corruption into the freedom of the glory of the children of God</u>. For we know that the whole creation groans and suffers the pains of childbirth together until now.

We have arrived at the time to set this world free from its slavery. It's time to put the devil under our feet. It's time to speak with the authority of God. And it's time to pray and fast so that revelation can be released from heaven to help us in troubled times. Because of <u>humanistic thinking</u> the world has sunk in such a mess, but <u>we</u> are <u>in</u> the world and <u>not</u> of this world!

When we enter into the Kingdom of God we begin to <u>think with kingdom mentality</u>. As a man thinks in his heart, so is he (Proverbs 23:7). A son thinks and acts like his father (if he is imitating his father). He does not wonder about his behavior or conduct. He is one with his father (John 17:21). As sons mature into their sonship they take on a greater responsibility to operate in their God-given rights. Yes, much is expected!

Over 2000 years ago God declared that this is the Churches' future glory – to enter into Sonship. Well, the future is now and it is our glory now! All creation groans inwardly for the remnant of God to arise and do His Will in the earth as it is in heaven. We are the sons of God now!

Isn't that an awesome thought – the world is waiting on us! They need us, because as God heard the groaning of His people in Abraham's day – He still hears today! God intends for us to take part in His plan of the restoration for all humanity. If He used Abraham in all his frailty, He will use us as well.

Exodus 2:24-25:

So God heard their groaning; and God remembered His covenant with Abraham, Isaac, and Jacob. And God saw the sons of Israel, and God took notice of them.

So let's rise up and do what we are called to do. Preach, teach, lay hands, cast out

<u>devils and heal the sick</u>! For the kingdom of heaven suffers violence, but the violent take it by force (Matthew 11:12).

Day 14

Wake Up – Don't Go Back to Sleep, the Holy
Spirit Has Something to Tell You

Lament. 2:19
**<u>Arise, cry out</u> in the night: in the beginning of
the watches <u>pour out thine heart</u> like water
before the face of the Lord: lift up thy hands
toward him <u>for the life of thy young children</u>
that faint for hunger in the top of every street.**

In order to pour out our hearts before
the Lord, we must be <u>deeply troubled</u> in our
spirits. Intolerable pain will only provoke a
man or a woman to change their surroundings;
because whatever they tolerate they cannot
change.

<u>Do a Diagnostic Test</u>: Have we become
disturbed enough over what we see and hear,
or have we become desensitized to the sin in
our nation? Do we yearn for the Lord in the
night season and do our spirits long for Him in
the morning to bask in His presence?

If we are not disturbed enough or
possess a lethargic attitude or believe "what
will be, will be," it is time to allow the Holy

Spirit to troubleshoot and make repairs in our attitude.

Desperate measures cause for desperate means: (1) Arise! Shake yourself – get up, don't go back to sleep…the Holy Spirit wants to reveal to us the secrets of the Kingdom. (2) Cry out - To pour out our heart means to feel helpless as Jesus was on the cross when He said, "Father, why hast thou forsaken me?" Jesus was sinless and He paid for our sin as He hung on that cross. Abba Father loves us so much that He went to desperate means to redeem His children back to Himself.

Will we go the extra mile and cry out for the souls of our children? It is only right for us to do so, because God has given our children to us as a gift and an inheritance.

Finally, don't let your hands grow limp or your eyes grow weary, because the Lord is powerful and strong…His powers unleash like a hailstorm and a destructive wind, able to drive any opposing force away from His people.

God will teach our hands to war. If His finger points to the target, His hand will make a way for us to hit and not miss.

Day 15
The Family's Business - Servanthood

Job 22:21
Acquaint now thyself with him, and be at peace: thereby good shall come unto thee.

Over the years, we have witnessed a progression of moral decay in our nation. Now we see the results. Decay takes time to reveal itself but before you know it, you feel excruciating pain that will not go away. Now we have to do something about the pain! The bad thing is that all the time we felt pain but we neglected it because it was just a nagging ache. We hoped it would go away or eventually work itself out.

Job 22:21 and countless other scriptures give us proven solutions to our problem. Just think, if we all came with a concerted effort to acquaint ourselves with the Almighty God, and make peace with Him – this nation could be turned around instantly. Whereas, the moral decay progresses over time, but good can come to us immediately!

But how bad do we want the peace of God? It will take a lot of effort to change, and change comes at a great price. We have become a <u>self-serving nation</u>, and it will take <u>dethroning the flesh</u>.

Jesus said that He came <u>not to be served but to serve</u>. To serve is to give your life for another. People need help and assistance, but we are too blind to see their needs because <u>we</u> are so needy ourselves.

The Bible says to pray to the Lord of the harvest that He may send forth workers (Matthew 9:38). I encourage you to pray this and I asked the Lord of the Harvest to give the workers <u>sight</u> to see the need. He waits for us to bombard heaven with the incense of our prayers. Remember, the Bible also says "What we decide on will be done, and light will shine on our way" (Job 22:28).

Day 16
Loose Them and Let Them Go

John 11:40
Jesus said to her, "Did I not say to you, if you believe, you will see the glory of God?"

Martha and Mary had just lost their brother, Lazarus. He had been <u>lying in a tomb with a stone rolled over the entrance for about four days, and had begun to stink</u>. They both felt that <u>if Jesus had been there</u> - their brother would not have died.

Lazarus represents the younger generation. We see that the majority of them are spiritually dead because of something someone said or some unfortunate circumstance, therefore they stink. However Jesus has given us the power to speak the Resurrection and Life over them, and <u>we don't have to wait until Jesus comes</u>.

Revelation 3:2 declares that we are to "Awake and strengthen the things that remain…" <u>We have the authority to act now</u>!

In the Greek, a stone was symbolized as a stumbling block, and/or an occasion to cause to fall. What do we speak over the younger generation? When we look at them we find it tempting to say things like: "I don't know what this generation is coming to!" "They are acting like idiots!" or "This generation is dying and going straight to hell!"

Well, these phrases take on the form of curses or stumbling blocks which prevent our young people from entering into the Kingdom of God. Therefore, they stay spiritually dead and stink until they die physically and stink. What we say is what we will end-up with!

Martha *focused* so much on the fact that Lazarus had been dead for quite some time, that she thought it impossible for her to see any immediate good come from it. She only believed that Lazarus would rise again in the resurrection on the last day. Martha represents the Church! Are we so *focused* on the forest that we can't see the tree…that it will turn out to be – a *strong oak*? Are we still waiting for Jesus to do something and hoping to see the result when we all get to heaven?

When Jesus called Lazarus out of the tomb, He told the people to "Loose him and let him go!" We can loose and free the next generation from the world's system with Words of life. Our right attitude will permit them to move about with divine purpose (their feet); work and take action (their hands); and the appearances of their face will shine as the brightness of day. <u>They will go and bring forth fruit</u>!

Jesus is the Resurrection and Life! He transcends death and destruction and any hopeless situation. Therefore, let's re-direct our attention to Him. We are in the <u>last days,</u> so let's continue to pray and believe until we see change! It may take a while but <u>if we believe in Him, we shall see the glory of God</u>.

Day 17
The Holy Spirit is With Us

Judges 4:6-8

And she (*Deborah*) sent and called Barak ...and said unto him, Hath not the LORD God of Israel commanded, *saying,* Go and draw toward mount Tabor, and take with thee ten thousand men of the children of Naphtali and of the children of Zebulun? And <u>I will draw unto thee ...the captain of Jabin's army,</u> with his chariots and his multitude; <u>and I will deliver him into thine hand. And Barak said unto her, If thou wilt go with me, then I will go: but if thou wilt not go with me,</u> *then* <u>I will not go.</u>

The Bible speaks of numerous accounts where God initiated the battle to redeem His people. It feels very uncomfortable when God calls you to break the code of ethics on <u>evil</u> when society says that <u>good is politically wrong. For people will call evil good and good evil</u> (Isaiah 5:20), and we now live out what was spoken by the prophet Isaiah.

In Judges 4:6-8, Deborah (who represented the Holy Spirit) was one of God's anointed-ones with the anointing. God set her in the position as judge and ruler because Israel had done evil for twenty years; therefore He sold them into the hand of the enemy. Now they cried out to the Lord for help.

Of course God wanted to use Barak (who represented the Church) to defeat the army of Jabin. However, for twenty years, Barak had grown cowardly and in contrast to Deborah, (who ruled with her faith) he had very little faith. I believe while the people hid from the enemy, Deborah hid in the presence of the Lord, her Strong Tower.

Thank God that He did not see Barak as Barak saw himself; rather He saw Barak as a mighty man who could defeat Israel's enemy no matter how high the odds. When God called Barak, He had already given him the victory.

Notice the significance of symbolism in these few scriptures. Barak (knowing his faith was weak) had enough sense to not to go into battle without Deborah. God will never send His people into battle without His Anointing. We don't have to fear our enemy - just be obedient to the call of God. Remember, obedience ranks as our greatest accomplishment!

We cannot stay in our comfort zone and play it safe anymore; the hour commands that we <u>come together as one body</u> and fight the battle <u>with</u> the Lord. He has assured us the <u>victory because the Holy Spirit dwells within us</u>!

Day 18

It's Time to PUSH

Galatians 4:19

But oh, my dear children! I feel as if I am going through <u>labor pains for you again</u>, and they will continue until Christ is fully developed in your lives.

Paul was writing to the Galatians. They had become his spiritual children because of their present faith in Jesus, the Christ. They were set free from the law and were now children of the promise. False teachers had infiltrated among the Galatians to lure them away from Paul in order to put them into bondage <u>again to the law</u>.

Paul became so burdened for the Galatians, and grieved in his spirit that it caused him to go into <u>labor pains and travail for their continual freedom in Christ</u>. He wanted them to experience the fullness of God's grace as heirs of the promise. Paul felt it necessary to confront them with the <u>truth</u> about the motives of these false teachers. However, the Galatians <u>now</u> considered Paul an <u>enemy</u>!

What a wonderful father! Paul felt such a responsibility towards the Galatians that he allowed himself to be burdened to the point of getting into the birthing position to <u>PUSH for their survival in the liberty of Christ</u>.

As it was then, so it is today! Many have been born again and become heirs of the kingdom; God's spirit lives in them, but the Christ life has been hindered from being fully developing.

Our responsibility rests to help those who act as babes to advance to maturity. It will <u>cost us time in prayer, a meal or two</u> and even <u>confronting with the truth</u> at times. Their souls depend on <u>our intercession</u>.

Every parent desires to see his/her child fully develop emotionally, physically and even spiritually. But do they claim it as a priority? Do we weep over them or do we just watch the enemy run circles around them?

Well, Paul took the bull by the horns at the risk of being labeled their enemy. Jesus did it also! We're running in good company, so let's do the same. As a medical doctor says PUSH... I can see the head; Jesus says, "<u>PUSH...I can see the transformation</u>"!

Day 19

Do You Hear the Sound of the Siren?

Joel 2:15
Blow the trumpet in Zion, sanctify a fast, call a solemn assembly:

Whenever we hear a siren, it lets us know that something is wrong. The sound of the siren can be just a warning or an alert that something is about to happen. It also means danger - some catastrophe has taken place and someone needs assistance. Whatever the case may be, the sound of the siren is needful and helpful but we must pay attention and give heed to its sound.

Sometimes when we hear it at a distance we tend to have a non-caring attitude and just continue with our routine. But when it gets closer, we give more attention to it and wonder, "What is wrong and who needs help?"

When we get caught in a traffic jam, and need to arrive someplace at a certain time, we get *annoyed* because we don't understand the reason for the *stand still*, until we hear the sound of the siren behind us in the distance. Then we and the other annoyed drivers try to maneuver our cars into lanes already jammed with cars.

We become annoyed because, we believe that what we have to do, and where we have to go, is more important than the disaster that we witness. Oh, some of us will offer up a prayer to God for <u>help</u> because it is our Christian duty.

A TV commercial showed two teens, one drowning in an ocean and the other standing on the board-walk <u>watching</u> his friend drown. Nothing was said or done in the commercial, and then you saw these words flash across the TV screen: "If you saw your friend drowning in drugs, would you go and help him?" According to the actions of the teen that watched, we could assume the answer was "no" or maybe the teen did not know what actions to take.

The sound of the siren will alert various types of trained personnel and equipment to the accident scene: Policemen, paramedics in an ambulance, and firefighters in a fire truck. These trained experts have given their lives as public servants to assist in accidents, no matter how menial or life threatening the situation. They have given an oath to <u>protect</u>!

We, as Christians, may not be out in the front where others can see us as these public servants, but God needs us in prayer as spiritual enforcers, paramedics, and firemen. We have the authority to change a situation and save a life.

The spiritual siren (or trumpet) has blown and now blows to get our attention. Let's take heed! If we look at what happens around us today, the sound blasts louder and louder, moving closer and closer into view. It's really not hard to see the sound!

Day 20

Wheat and Tares

Matthew 13:25, 30
But while men slept, his enemy came and sowed tares among the wheat, and went his way…Let both grow together until the harvest: and in the time of harvest I will say to the reapers, Gather ye together first the tares, and bind them in bundles to burn them: but gather the wheat into my barn.

I dreamt of large tomato vines in my front yard. Some of the tomatoes were humongous and very red. Others had not quite developed yet. With two hands I proceeded to pluck one of the overgrown tomatoes which was very ripe and looked delicious. When I opened it with my two thumb fingers it had a mushy appearance inside. It did not appeal to the eye so I did not want to eat it.

The Holy Spirit revealed to me that "the difference between the wheat and tare is what is <u>inside</u>. Just because someone has a big ministry, drives a nice car, is financially blessed and lives in a big house, does not necessarily mean that he has the <u>character of God</u>. Many Christians in the Body of Christ resemble the humongous tomatoes on the vine but remain <u>hollow inside</u>. They have no real substance!"

I proceeded to ask the Holy Spirit, "How did they get to be like that if we all have a salvation experience and are a part of the Body of Christ?" The Holy Spirit reminded me of a lesson taught on how to determine if a tree is healthy or not. When a tree has vines or branches wrapped around it, the life in the tree is being sucked out of it by the parasite. Therefore, it could easily lift the unhealthy tree from its roots.

Matthew 13:22

He also that received seed among the thorns is he that heareth the word; and the care of this world, and the deceitfulness of riches, choke the word, and he becometh unfruitful.

Lastly, as we think of tares, most of us don't want any involvement with them because they do not bear fruit, so we shun them, or disassociate ourselves with them. But Jesus says to let them grow together until the last day when the angels will separate them. But I heard the Spirit of Grace say to me, "Don't shun or disc the tares because somewhere in the process, <u>they may be</u>

<u>influenced by your life and become wheat</u>!" So let's pray that we have an impact in our sphere of influence.

Day 21

The Power of Vision

Proverbs 29:18
Where *there is* no vision, the people perish:
but he that keepeth the law, happy *is* he.

The word *vision* means to set one's sight into <u>the future</u>. Other interchangeable terms are purpose, objectives, tasks, goals or mission statement. In other words, a vision can be future objectives and goals that you set for yourself, family, business or ministry.

A vision can come in many forms - a dream, prophecy, revelation, or an oracle, and many times applies to the <u>distant future</u>. Whatever form, it is from the mind (heart) of God! The Bible says, "Man shall not live by bread (his appetite) alone, but by every word (revelation) from the mouth (mind) of God." A mental sight from God will cause dead things to live and an almost dead thing to revive.

Not having a vision will cause a people to be destroyed or ruined. However, having one will produce the opposite effect. The power of a vision will help you stay on track and not deviate from the path that God has set before you. It will give you light when it's dark, peace among confusion and hope in despair. It also helps you to stay disciplined and not run wild.

For years, I had no concept of what God wanted me to do. I was fully aware that I was created for a purpose but I had not yet tapped into it. So I would try all sorts of things, hoping I would hit the jack-pot! But, when God revealed the vision to me and I was able to <u>see it</u> – then I had faith to <u>bring the vision to pass</u>.

Take for instance, the account of Elizabeth and Mary (read Luke 1). Elizabeth had been barren all her life, but she and her husband had a vision that one day God would remove her reproach and bless them with a child. And that day came! The womb that was once barren now carried the forerunner for the Messiah to make ready a people for His coming.

One the other hand, Mary had never known a man and was now pregnant by the Holy Spirit with the Son of God. What a phenomenal miracle. The child that she carried in her womb would be the Savior of the world.

Here we see two ordinary women with a vision inside of them that would have a major impact in the entire world for generations to come. Both of them had to go through all kinds of ridicule and stigma! But these visions had so much <u>power </u>that at <u>the appointed time, God revealed them</u>.

So be encouraged, if you are not walking in your God-give vision yet, it is for an appointed time. It can stay hidden only the time allotted by God. It is too powerful, and God will not deny Himself. <u>Reposition yourself and set your eyes on what you see</u>!

Day 22

Stay Conscious
(Part 1)

Hebrews 2:1
We must pay more attention, therefore to what we have heard, so that we do not drift away. (NIV)

We can discover two kinds of people in the earth: sober and drunk. A sober person stays aware of his environment. He considers who, what, why, when, where and how a situation affects the kingdom. This person discerns the times.

On the other hand, the drunken person is self consumed with getting the next fix to gratify his or her appetite. He also considers: Who is going to help *me*, what about *me*, why *me*, when is it going to happen for *me*, where am *I* going to go and how am *I* going to do something? It is all about him! We have all fallen into this category from time to time.

Nevertheless, God keeps reminding us to "stay conscious, pay attention, be on the alert and be watchful." We have to practice to stay conscious, because we get hit and side tracked with stuff every day. The days are evil and it will only get worse.

On many occasions as I talked with a person, I was not really attentive to what he said. Rather I waited for him to take a breath in order to express my opinion on the subject matter. As such I operated as a *pretender*! Pretenders are people whose eyes are locked on the person or something but their mind has drifted far away. They do not really listen, because their thoughts distract them.

Then we run into the *selective* people, who zoom in and out. They go in and out of consciousness. I have witnessed this with many of our youth who reject what they don't want to hear. They have honed this technique down to an art which is the way that they communicate.

Fortunately, we cherish the *focus* people, who lock in and hang onto every word that we speak. They are in a conscious state! They don't plan on what to say, because they listen for the voice of the Holy Spirit to speak a *now word* in the situation.

Which one are you? It's time to evaluate our position spiritually. God wants us to stay alert and not drift away when He speaks to us. It's for our protection! **1 Peter 5:8** states, "Be of sober *spirit,* be on the alert. Your adversary, the devil, prowls about like a roaring lion, seeking someone to devour."

Day 23

Shhh!

(Part 2)

Job 4:16

It stood still, but I could not discern the form thereof: an image _was_ before mine eyes, _there was_ silence, and I heard a voice, _saying,_

Have you ever wanted to talk to people and they were either on the cell phone, the computer, playing their iPod, watching TV or text-messaging a friend. What you had to say was very important! But you had to wait your turn. These parties see you in their view but they are so distracted by their own activity that they cannot discern your need. Soon you get tired of waiting or your attempts to communicate prove pointless, so you eventually walk away.

What I have just described we find typical of our modern society in which we live. In this technocratic age we have become mass media addicts! The sad thing about the multi-media technology is that we need it to accomplish our work, find out what's going on in the world, and to contact friends or relatives.

We have become so inundated with the use of the media that it consumes every waking minute of our day. Even more devastating, we have cursed our children. When they see us spending all our time engaged in today's mass-media, they easily follow suit.

Job says that the Spirit stood before him but he could not discern Him because there was <u>so much noise</u> that it distorted his perception to <u>see and hear</u>. Not until there was silence, did he <u>hear the voice of the Spirit</u>.

God is always speaking but we fail to listen. He won't shout, and He won't continue to stand before us and be put on hold or tolerate our rudeness. We have all been guilty of this, yet it would disturb us, even make us mad if God treated us in this manner.

1 Kings 19:12 states, "And after the earthquake a fire; *but* the LORD *was* not in the fire: and after the fire a still small voice." We won't hear His voice until we get rid of the noise. God wants to talk to us; are we ready to listen?

Be still, and know that I *am* God: I will be exalted among the heathen, I will be exalted in the earth **(Psalm 46:10).**

Day 24

The Day – The Earth Stood Still
(Part 3)

Habakkuk 2:20
But the LORD *is* in his holy temple: let all the earth keep silence before him.

When my pastor asked the congregation to join-in a 21 day fast, I had to seek the Lord as to what I was to give up. Food is not a big problem for me because I am a vegan. I juice in the morning and eat very light during lunch and dinner.

I wanted to give up something that would really be a sacrifice unto the Lord and a discipline to my flesh. I believe the Spirit of the Lord said to give up TV and the radio. I have the radio on all the time and I usually watch TV at least three hours each evening, valuable time that I could well spend doing something much more constructive.

Well, I took the challenge, and on the first day, I would reach to turn on the radio or think about what was going to be on my favorite sitcom. This went on for a couple of days the first week and even into the second week until I finally got used to enjoying the silence. I would pray, read the Bible or continue to write this book (which you are reading now).

I noticed a couple of things: I could hear God more clearly, I had the inspiration to write which helped me to perfect my gift and I was less stressed. I simply enjoyed the presence of God.

Today's multi-media industry has taken us on a long journey; therefore we have become tired and restless. But Jesus says, "Come unto me and I will give you rest"(Matthew 11:28).

What would happen if we all would fast from TV, cell phones, computers, iPods, and radios for one day, and instead, pray, spend time with friends and family, read a book, write a hand written letter, ride a bike or go on a nature walk? How would we feel? Would we feel less important, useless, or would we run and hide because then we would have to come face to face with God.

Habakkuk says the Lord is in His holy temple and we are the temple of the Lord! Our flesh, which comes from the earth, has strived against its Maker since the day sin entered the world. Instead of us being Spirit ruled we allow our flesh to rule. Yet we have the power in us to speak peace to our restlessness. God beckons to us to return to Him. He wants to lead us to green pastures where we will find rest for our weary souls beside the still waters (Read Psalm 23). Right now the waters are rough, disturbing and agitating.

Since I have been on this fast, the earth has stood still <u>for me</u>. You can cause your earth to stand still as well. I don't ever want to be <u>guilty again</u> of saying what Jacob said when he awoke out of his sleep… "Surely the LORD is in this place; and <u>I knew *it* not</u>" (**Genesis 28:16**).

When we sleep, we are in a state of un-consciousness. Whatever causes us to be unconscious, be it TV, Internet, radio or iPods, we need to sacrifice it on the altar until we control our activity instead of it controlling us. <u>Take the challenge and cause your earth to stand still</u>!

Day 25

Keep Vigil

Exodus 12:42
Because the LORD **kept <u>vigil</u> that night <u>to bring them out of Egypt</u>, on this night all the Israelites are to keep <u>vigil</u> to honor the Lord for <u>the generations to come</u>. (NIV)**

The word vigil means *a day of spiritual preparation before a religious feast.* In the above scripture text, the religious feast was the Passover where God prepared His people to come out of a life of bondage in Egypt. God also established this vigil as a memorial in honor of Himself and one that God instructed the Israelites to keep for generations to come.

The Amplified version says it was a <u>night</u> of watching and to be much <u>celebrated</u> by the Israelites for God bringing them out of Egypt. At night usually everything ceases and we sleep. Contrary to this natural pattern, the spirit world remains constantly active. Our enemy never sleeps!

Exodus 12:42
It was a night of watching unto the Lord and to be much observed for bringing them out of Egypt; this same night of watching unto the

Lord is to be observed by all the Israelites throughout their generations. (Amplified)

Even though God had already pre-determined the Israelites' deliverance (Genesis 15:12-15) and brought them out with a strong arm, the enemy would not give up that easily. Therefore, God kept watch over His word to perform it (Jeremiah 1:12). He spoke it and He cannot lie (Titus 1:2).

The Lord tells us today to have a special celebration for our deliverance (Jesus Christ, our Passover Lamb) as an everlasting ordinance. Isn't it ironic - God has designed the body to sleep at night, yet now He tells us this is a time to go without sleep but watch and celebrate your deliverance in honor of Me. God wants not only our generation but the generations to follow, to practice this ordinance.

If we do not keep vigil, how will the next generation know? God commanded the older generation to rehearse His deeds and acts to their children that they might observe and know the Lord God.

Lastly, when we keep vigil it benefits the generations to come. We pray as well as watch for their souls, that they may come out of the world's system and inherit their promised land. We turn the battle at the gate and declare life by speaking the decrees of the Lord into the spirit realm.

We consider it an honor to keep vigil with the Lord. So many spiritual blessings take place that we don't recognize. But if we will not tire in the night vigil, we shall reap an abundant harvest that will affect our children, their children and their children's children!

Day 26

If God is My Lover...Then Why Is My Bed So Cold?

Song 5:2-3, 6
I sleep, but my heart waketh: *it is* **the voice of my beloved that knocketh,** *saying,* **Open to me, my sister, my love, my dove, my undefiled: for my head is filled with dew,** *and* **my locks with the drops of the night. I have put off my coat; how shall I put it on? I have washed my feet; how shall I defile them? ...I opened to my beloved; but my beloved had withdrawn himself,** *and* **was gone: my soul failed when he spake: I sought him, but I could not find him; I called him, but he gave me no answer.**

When I go to bed at night, my room and bed are very cold, so cold that I wear socks to bed year around. Fortunately, my bed is layered with many blankets, and it takes a while before my body adjusts to the crisp coolness of the sheets. After tossing and turning continually to get the blood flowing in my body to generate body heat, I can rest comfortably.

I get agitated with myself if I forget to do something before retiring for the night. I wait and contemplate if I want to pull back the covers and get out of the bed to do something that I would rather put off until morning. Therefore, I lie there for several minutes before forcing myself out of a semi-warm bed.

Well, many of us have spiritual beds that reflect what I have just described. Our hearts grow so cold towards God, yet He wants to once again ignite the flames of our affection for Him. Unfortunately, we have become too tired from the day's chores: working 8-10 hours, preparing family dinner, bathing the children, making school lunches, and trying to keep afloat with our own personal issues. Soon the once hot passion for the Lord fizzles out to lukewarm.

The Lord always comes to sup with us for He wants to commune with His people. In the account of creation, God made everything good. It was so good that He said let us make man in our image and likeness so that he can enjoy the good that I have created. Therefore, God's ultimate reason for creating man was and is for fellowship.

Yet it seems that God comes to fellowship at the most inconvenient time.

During the day we are too busy He cannot get our attention, therefore, He comes when it's quiet and we sit at rest. However, we feel too tired so we make all kinds of excuses for not spending time with Him.

God is not interested in a brief casual encounter. Rather He desires an intimate relationship and wants to stay indefinitely. How bad do we want Him? He aims to please, but are we ready to receive what He has to offer? John 10:10 says, "... I am come that they might have life, and that they might have *it* more abundantly."

The scripture text talks about dew, which is symbolic of freshness. The Lover knew that the woman was tired and exhausted, and He wanted to refresh her. She was so focused on her present situation that she missed out on her future opportunity to experience the kisses and the caresses of her Lover, therefore He departed.

Is your bed cold? Well, it doesn't have to be, because the Lover is knocking on the door of your heart...invite Him in! Jesus says, "Behold, I stand at the door, and knock: if any man hears my voice, and opens the door, I will come in to him, and will sup with him, and he with me" (Rev. 3:20).

Day 27

I Was Good as Dead

Ephesians 2:4-5
But God, who is rich in mercy, for his great love wherewith he loved us, even when we were dead in sins, hath quickened us together with Christ, (by grace ye are saved).

In 1982, on a fall night, as I drove on Interstate 95, I was hit from behind by an eighteen wheeler. At the point of contact, the impact threw my car into a spin. My car traveled across four lines of traffic during rush hour; hitting the barrier which then caused my car to turn in the opposite direction, hitting another car head-on before it came to a complete stop.

The accident jerked my body all out of sorts and the blow to the head generated a constant pulsation and a protruding knot. When they helped me out of my car, I was in a state of shock and not coherent as to what really happened. The accident caused every lane of traffic to come to a stand-still. "I should have died!"

My initial reaction was spontaneous; Praise and worship! I lifted up my hands to the

Lord and repeated over and again, "Thank you Jesus"! I was not concerned about who saw or heard me! I was as good as dead… but God, rich in mercy overrode the enemy's counsel and delivered me from a destined fate.

This accident parallels my life before Christ. I was living in my sins and trespasses, traveling on the road to hell. The road to hell is wide and it leads only to destruction (Matthew 7:13-14). My life resembled a spinning top whirling in all kinds of directions, having head-on collisions and causing all kinds of rifts. I was battered mentally and torn emotionally, having no hope and living an empty life.

I was as good as dead, because the enemy had a field day in my life. But all things worked together for my good, for God turned the situation around in my life. He used all my pain and suffering to arouse my awareness that I needed Him, thus bringing me to saving grace in Jesus Christ.

When it was my time to enter into the kingdom of His marvelous light, God stopped all of the devil's trafficking and delivered me from death's door. I rejoice today! That past experience in the natural reminds me that I was as good as dead, but God, rich in mercy and His great love for me, made me alive together with Christ, (<u>by grace I am saved</u>).

What's in your past that will cause you to <u>rejoice about your today</u>?

Day 28

The Law of Attraction

Job 3:25
For the thing which I greatly feared is come upon me, and that which I was afraid of is come unto me.

What is on your mind lately? The Bible declares that if your mind is stayed on God you will remain in <u>perfect peace</u> (Isaiah 26:3).

Job had a fear that was <u>deep seated</u> in him. He may not have talked about it, but it was resident in his life, always in the back of his mind. He continually demonstrated it when he offered sacrifices up to the Lord always thinking... "Perhaps my sons have sinned and cursed God in their hearts." Thus Job did continually (Job 1:5).

What we give audience to, we strengthen and give life. When you sow a seed, it has the potential to become a tree, and the tree has the potential to become a forest.

What do you attract to yourself? Is it peace, righteousness, joy and prosperity, or is it fear, lack, and poverty? Occasionally, we are not conscience of our thoughts. Our grandmothers and mothers thought a certain way so we think in the same manner. The Bible holds true when it says that whatever we think in our heart, so are we (Proverbs 23:7).

I am persuaded that if we think on <u>God,</u> <u>everything that is of God</u> will be attracted to us. The negative to the positive thinking concept is - <u>without God,</u> it is just a good thought verses a God thought.

The God of peace wants to establish peace around our borders so that the enemy will not come near them. Our peace then will resemble flowing rivers in the midst of disaster and turmoil. All those within our borders will also experience that peace because the Prince of Peace will dwell among His people.

So let's do what Philip. 4:8 says, **"Finally, brethren, whatsoever things are true, whatsoever things *are* honest, whatsoever things *are* just, whatsoever things *are* pure, whatsoever things *are* lovely, whatsoever things *are* of good report; if *there be* any virtue, and if *there be* any praise, think on these things."** If we practice what the Apostle Paul preaches, watch and see what attracts us – the Kingdom of Heaven!

Day 29

The Place of Spiritual Decompression

Psalm 91:1
He that dwelleth in the secret place of the most High shall abide under the shadow of the Almighty.

We now reap results of past sins committed by our ancestors. They affect us on a social and economic level. Some of it affects us on a personal level but the majority is nation wide. Hurricanes, tornados, floods, fires, wars, isolated beatings and killings are just a few, and a few too many.

We have come to the point individually and corporately that we don't know what to do. We have called in all kinds of experts and tried so many tactics, that we have become totally confused and wonder... "What next?" Well, the pressure is on and it won't let up any time soon!

Psalm 91 is a familiar text that most of us can quote in part if not in its entirety. David wrote this Psalm when he was running from his enemies (the pressures of life). The psalmist knew that if he could just get to the secret place and dwell there, he would be safe because his enemy could not find him.

The word "dwell" means to live or abide. Where? In the secret place or another translation says in the shadow of the Most High. This psalm implies that if you just get there you can abide. The issue here is getting to the secret place. The pressures of life can so burden us down, distract us and choke the life out of us that we forget that we have a fortress or hidden place we can retreat to and stay there.

Mark 4:19

And the cares of this world, and the deceitfulness of riches, and the lusts of other things entering in, choke the word, and it becometh unfruitful.

Another interesting word is "shadow". In order to get into someone's shadow you have to be close to him and a shadow is produced only by light. God is light and He will shine light on our understanding. The revelation we should receive is that being in His presence or secret place ranks more important than the pressures of life we now face.

We may have to practice going in and out of the presence of God until we learn to remain there. However, once we become conscious of the daily distractions and pit falls that the enemy sets in our view, we will soon ignore him and his devilish antics.

The secret place - where the presence of God is - is the place where decompression takes place. The Bible says that those (the righteous) who run into the Strong Tower are safe. What will it take for you to run into the secret place and abide there?

Day 30

Hush!

1 Chronicles 16:22
"Do not touch My anointed ones, and do My prophets no harm." (NASB)

The word touch in the Hebrew means to smite, beat, strike; to reach; or to inflict plagues, on someone or something. When we speak ill of the men or women of God and their ministry, we are striking them with **words which are spirit** (John 6:63). Words can bless or curse!

Usually when we become offended, dissatisfied and disgruntled, we express our feelings to others that do not need to know about the problem. We should <u>first</u> go to the offended person to make things right. Only when the two parties can't settle the issue, do we seek after a third party (an elder of the Church). It is biblical and Jesus said it!

Matthew 18:15-16
Moreover if thy brother shall trespass against thee, go and tell him his fault <u>between thee and him alone</u>: if he shall hear thee, thou hast gained thy brother. But if he will not hear

thee, then take with thee one or two more, that in the mouth of two or three witnesses every word may be established.

As I have matured in my Christian walk, when I hear people quote 1 Chronicles 16:22, the fear of God rises up in me to take it more seriously than I did before. The repercussions of disobeying this command as well as all of God's commands can damage your health and spiritual walk.

One thing that happened to me is that I could not hear the voice of God, which is vital to my daily spiritual intake. I can not live by my appetite alone; I need to hear from God. A person with an appetite – if they are not being fed in the natural will soon die. First the natural – then the spiritual (1 Corinthians 15:46).

Genesis 20:7
"Now therefore, restore the man's wife, for he is a prophet, and he will pray for you, and you will live. But if you do not restore *her*, know that you shall surely die, you and all who are yours." (NASB)

Eventually everything dies – your dreams, ministry, as well as individual and family goals. The death on the inside of you will even manifest itself in your body through sickness. You may even believe that you are hearing from God, but it is your own voice/flesh or a demonic spirit. You therefore open the door to the kingdom of darkness!

Remember, there is no perfect Church, because there are no perfect people; only one perfect love – "agape". So let's try to make allowances for each other's mistakes. God did!

And just a word of advice; if you don't go to your offended brother or sister and work out the situation…just "<u>hush</u>," because it's not worth the judgment that you bring on yourself!

Day 31

What's In Your Hand?

Matthew 25:14-15
For *the kingdom of heaven is* **as a man travelling into a far country,** *who* **called his own servants, and delivered unto them his goods. And unto one he gave five talents, to another two, and to another one; to every man according to his several ability; and straightway took his journey.**

The problem today remains to find out what is in a man's hand or what his or her gift is. God gives talent to all His servants and expects a return on His investment. Each believer must discover his God-given gift or seed. Thereafter the believer can multiply, replenish and subdue the earth with his gift.

Our gift is always in seed form. When we don't know about and understand the gift God has given us, we can abuse it. We examine several reasons why people abuse seed-gifts:

1) Ignorance. Hosea 4:6 states that **"My people are destroyed for lack of knowledge"**. It is impossible to utilize something if you do not know what you

have. Better yet, when we don't know the purpose of a thing, the propensity to abuse becomes inevitable.

2) The fear of putting the seed to use. The servant in Matthew 25 hid his talent, the reason Jesus called him wicked and lazy. Operating in fear will cause us to despise the gift.

3) Inadequacies. Moses and Gideon stands out as two examples:

Exodus 4:10, Then Moses said to the Lord, "Please, Lord, I have never been eloquent, neither recently nor in time past, nor since Thou hast spoken to Thy servant; for I am slow of speech and slow of tongue." (NASB)

Judges 6:15, And he (Gideon) said to Him, "O Lord, how shall I deliver Israel? Behold, my family is the least in Manasseh, and I am the youngest in my father's house." (NASB)

Moses had a shepherd stick in his hand therefore it became the staff of God. In like manner God can perform miracles with whatever a man has in his hand. In our weakness God manifest His strength.

4) Not being diligent. Laziness and procrastination stands out as enormous hindrances which keep people from turning their seed and stirring up their gift. Paul tells

Timothy to stir up his gift; cause it to be active. Proverbs 6: 6-11 gives instructions about being wise like the ant while strongly rebuking the sluggard. **"Go to the ant, O sluggard, observe her ways and be wise, which, having no chief, officer or ruler, prepares her food in the summer, and gathers her provision in the harvest. How long will you lie down, O sluggard? When will you arise from your sleep? "A little sleep, a little slumber, a little folding of the hands to rest"-- and your poverty will come in like a vagabond, and your need like an armed man." (NASB)**

<u>Ecclesiastes 11:6</u>, **"Sow your seed in the morning, and do not be idle in the evening, for you do not know whether morning or evening sowing will succeed, or whether both of them alike will be good." (NASB)** Every man is without an excuse because he can do all things in the strength of Christ. <u>Now, what is in your hand</u>? If you don't know, ask God, if you do, <u>be productive</u>. What you do with your seed can influence your future!

Day 32

Be Fruitful

(Part 2)

Genesis 1:28

And God blessed them, and God said unto them, Be fruitful, and multiply, and replenish the earth, and subdue it: and have dominion over the fish of the sea, and over the fowl of the air, and over every living thing that moveth upon the earth.

The first law of productivity is to "be fruitful." Fruitful is defined as the act of producing. Everyone has in his DNA the propensity to produce. The law of productivity is also called "the law of sowing and reaping" The Bible states that God gives seed to sow to produce a harvest.

We need to put to work the seed-gift we have within us. We call it a seed-gift, because the seed is a gift from God as opposed to having earned it. Conversely, we cannot sow another man's seed and expect to reap a harvest. Everyone has a different seed than others and should not despise it.

Some examples of seed-gifts include teacher, administrator, server, giver, and so forth. The Bible states that Esau despised his birthright and gave it up for a measly meal. Afterward he sought for it with tears because it cost him the blessing of the firstborn.

"And Esau said, "Behold, I am about to die; so of what use then is the birthright to me?" And Jacob said, "First swear to me"; so he swore to him, and sold his birthright to Jacob. Then Jacob gave Esau bread and lentil stew; and he ate and drank, and rose and went on his way. Thus Esau despised his birthright." (Genesis 25:32-34, NASB)

Our seed-gift has the potential to be fruitful and affect our entire life. Everything necessary to accomplish the will of God dwells inside us in seed form. The seed grows from inside out. Do not despise small beginnings. The mustard seed is the smallest seed and has the ability to produce an abundant harvest if sowed in faith. All seed gifts must be sowed in faith so that we expect a harvest.

He (Jesus) presented another parable to them, saying, **"The kingdom of heaven is like a mustard seed, which a man took and sowed in his field; and this is smaller than all other seeds; but when it is full grown, it is larger than the garden plants, and becomes a tree, so that the birds of the AIR come and nest in its** branches." **(Matthew 13:31-32, NASB)** To "be fruitful" is a mandate from God and not just some nice thing to do. <u>Are you fruitful</u>?

Day 33
Multiply
(Part 3)

Genesis 1:28
And God blessed them, and God said unto them, Be fruitful, and <u>multiply,</u> and replenish the earth, and subdue it: and have dominion over the fish of the sea, and over the fowl of the air, and over every living thing that moveth upon the earth.

The second law of productivity is multiplication which we define as "to excel and expand". Now that we have discovered and mastered the seed-gift we must increase it. **2 Corinthians 9:10, "Now He who supplies seed to the sower and bread for food, will supply and multiply your seed for sowing and increase the harvest of your righteousness." (NASB)**

A fashion designer creates a dress that becomes a masterpiece. To continue to make it by hand would be tedious and time consuming. Moreover, the designer would lose profit because the supply would not meet the demand. Therefore, it would limit the potential to multiply.

In our society many entrepreneurs have discovered and mastered their seed-gift, however they have ceased to advance to the next level to excel and expand. They operate in a habitual behavior - even though circumstances have changed and demand has increased, they become self-satisfied and complacent in just being fruitful. This technocratic age demands an increase in knowledge to keep up with current events. When we increase in knowledge, we increase our value.

Take for instance Microsoft; it started out with a basic word processing program. Presently it has a package with Excel, Power Point, Outlook, Recovery Application, Imaging and Scanning Application, Shortcut Bar Language Setting and much more. Every so often, Microsoft offers an updated version on its software.

One plants, one waters, and God is in the business of multiplying! Where are you in the process of productivity?

Day 34

Replenish the Earth
(Part 4)

Genesis 1:28
And God blessed them, and God said unto them, Be fruitful, and multiply, and <u>replenish the earth</u>, and subdue it: and have dominion over the fish of the sea, and over the fowl of the air, and over every living thing that moveth upon the earth.

The third law of productivity is replenish and is defined as *"to fill up;"* does the seed-gift impact and influence the world in a positive way?

<u>Psalm 72:17-19</u>
His name shall endure for ever: his name shall be continued as long as the sun: and *men* shall be blessed in him: all nations shall call him blessed. Blessed *be* the LORD God, the God of Israel, who only doeth wondrous things. And blessed *be* his glorious name for ever: and let the whole earth be filled *with* his glory; Amen, and Amen.

<u>Numbers 14:21</u>
But *as* truly *as* I live, all the earth shall be filled with the glory of the LORD.

God's purpose for this world is to be filled with His glory. He gave us a Multiple-choice quiz: Life or Death and He was gracious enough to also give us the answer, "<u>choose life</u>." We consider it wonderful that God would choose us to be co-laborers with Him to release His glory in the earth. Our seed-gift is not just limited to the church, but it is to impact the world.

Betha Mason excelled as a famous rap artist. The younger generation knew him by his impressive logo, "Ma$e" with the dollar sign. That catchy logo spoke of money, lots of money. Millions of youth worldwide liked his rap music. By his seed-gift he wrote lyrics about real life struggles which he put to music. He filled the earth through his music; however it was not for God. Rather Betha Mason released death because his rap music focused on sex, drugs, murder, and destruction.

Presently, he is saved, preaching the Word of God, pastoring a church and singing Christian rap music. Secular radio stations now play his music. Betha Mason now fills the earth with God's glory.

The first shall be last and the last shall be first! It is our time to take the lead and influence the world instead of the world influencing us with their vain imaginations. To God be the Glory!

Day 35

Subdue the Earth and have Dominion
(Part 5)

Genesis 1:28
And God blessed them, and God said unto them, Be fruitful, and multiply, and replenish the earth, <u>and subdue it: and have dominion</u> over the fish of the sea, and over the fowl of the air, and over every living thing that moveth upon the earth.

The fourth law of productivity is "<u>to subdue the earth</u>." To subdue the earth is defined as "to keep under, to rule, to conquer or to control." The Bible states that the earth is the Lord's and He has given it to man to have dominion. God wants to rule in the earth through us.
Psalm 115:16, "The heavens are the heavens of Jehovah, but the earth hath he given to the children of men."

Jesus instructs His disciple to pray "Thy Kingdom come thy will be done on earth as it is in heaven" (Matthew 6:10). God desires His way of doing things to be the standard in man's affairs, circumstances and the environment. God does not base His way of doing things on this world's beliefs and philosophies.

Jesus said that His kingdom is not of this world, because 1 Corinthians 1:27-29 states, **"But God hath chosen the foolish things of the world to confound the wise; and God hath chosen the weak things of the world to confound the things which are mighty; And base things of the world, and things which are despised, hath God chosen, *yea,* and things which are not, to bring to nought things that are: That no flesh should glory in his presence."**

If man functions successfully in the four laws of productivity, his seed-gift should affect the economic system nationally and internationally.

Oprah Winfrey shines as a very good example of this. As a humanitarian her objective is to inform her public audience of relevant issues that may affect them, be they adverse or positive. Because she operates in the four laws of productivity she is the richest and most influential woman in the twenty-first century who helps communities, countries and nations.

Oprah is not the only mover and shaker that God created in the earth. I believe I am one also – what about you?

Day 36

How bad do You Want Him?

Genesis 32:26
And he said, Let me go, for the day breaketh.
And he said, I will not let thee go, except thou
bless me.

We should come to a point in our life when we willingly give up everything to enjoy the presence of God. At that point you don't want anything else but Him. You have come to realize that your friends, family, money, job and status in society just aren't working anymore. They supported you in your need, and that was good then, but now you crave a force that transcends all of who and what you are.

You have accomplished many things in life – academic degrees, husband, wife, and family, a good job, and you even like the people you work with. However, you are longing for more. And you know that what you long for you will not find in this world, because if it was, you would have had it by now.

By the world's standard, Jacob was already successful – a good business man. He had two wives, many children, menservants, maidservants, cattle, donkeys, sheep, and goats. <u>What more could he want</u>? But he lived in fear because of his past behavior of trickery and deceit, and now he had to come face to face with it. Nothing that he had accomplished could give him a clean break from his past life.

Now Jacob was all alone with God. He had no human advisors, no wife to cuddle up with, no child's –play and no animal noises to distract him. He was desperate for God, therefore he was willing to wrestle all night and into the breaking of day to get the blessing of God. Jacob was at his wits end and he wanted God as much as the air that he breathed!

David stands out as another example. He was king – rich and successful, <u>but he wanted God's presence</u> more than all the riches in the world. His first attempt to move the ark of God into the city of David was a failure. He did not move the ark according to God's pattern and the Lord's wrath broke out against them - killing Uzzah. (Read 2 Samuel 6) Therefore, David was angry and afraid of the Lord that day.

Instead, the ark was taken to the house of Obed-Edom and remained there three months. The report got back to David that the presence of God was blessing Obed-Edom, his entire household, and everything he owned.

David was now willing to follow God's pattern to get the ark of God to come to him. 2 Samuel 6:16 says, that as the ark of God was entering into the city, David was beside himself – he leaped, danced, twirled, spun, and jumped with joy. He also offered burnt and fellowship offerings. David was willing to be undignified, and he humiliated himself for the presence of God (v. 23).

Here we read the account of two men who not only desired, or wanted, but needed the presence of God. They reacted totally different from each other but, they sought after the same thing - the presence of God…God Himself! One risked being alone with God; the other risked being a fool for God. What lengths will you take, to get the presence of God!

Day 37

Speak Boldly

Ephes. 6:19-20
...and *pray* **on my behalf, that utterance may be given to me in the opening of my mouth, to make known with boldness the mystery of the gospel, for which I am an ambassador in chains; that in** *proclaiming* **it I may speak boldly, as I ought to speak.**

Amendment I - Congress shall make no law respecting an establishment of religion, or prohibiting the free exercise thereof; or abridging the freedom of speech, or of the press; or the right of the people peaceably to assemble, and to petition the government for a redress of grievances.

While we still have the opportunity to speak freely about the gospel, let's do it! Many people look for the Truth to help them succeed in life, yet many people still grope in the dark because of erroneous doctrine from the past and from modern heresy.

The Church haters really push for the hate crime bill to become law. If this happens,

Christians will not be able to speak against sin as it relates to God, in risk of being sued or put in jail.

Paul's message to us encourages us to pray that God give us utterances to proclaim to those that desire and need to hear the gospel. Yes, the world wants to shut us up, but we still have the chance to speak; therefore, <u>let us seize every opportunity to do so</u>.

In Acts 4:17-20, people threatened the apostles Peter and John to not speak in the name of Jesus. "But Peter and John answered and said unto them, whether it be right in the sight of God to hearken unto you more than unto God, judge ye" (v. 19).

Various groups in our modern society take the first amendment out of context. They feel they can speak any ill words against the Church, and Jesus Christ, that it is acceptable. However, if the Church stands up for Christ and against sin in the world, we are criticized and accused of violating the first amendment.

We have to take the stance of the apostles. God stands ready to speak through many of us - let Him have His way. Proverbs 28:1 says that the righteous are as bold as a lion.

Day 38

Just for a Moment!

John 16:19, 22
"... A little while, and ye shall not see me: and again, a little while, and ye shall see me? And ye now therefore have sorrow: but I will see you again, and your heart shall rejoice, and your joy no man taketh from you."

We live in a world of unknowing and uncertainty. The President, the government, the experts and even the physicists fear in bewilderment of what to expect next. Everyone prophesies peace and safety, but Jesus has said we will experience much grief, but just for a moment. **2 Peter 3:8** declares that one day *is* with the Lord as a thousand years, and a thousand years as one day. God has even cut short the day of sorrow for the elect's sake (Matthew 24:22).

If we can hold out just for a moment and not weary in well-doing we will see Jesus' second coming for when He comes, we will have everlasting joy. However, while we wait we can still rejoice...rejoice in the fact that Jesus is coming back for His Bride.

Jesus compares our grief to a pregnant woman in labor which can be for an extended period of time. Fortunately, at the time of birth, if there are no complications, it takes just a moment to deliver. Once the baby arrives, the mother is happy with glee because the birth pains have ceased.

Likewise, with our present sufferings – which are just for a moment and cannot be compared to the eternal weight of glory that we can expect (2 Corinthians 4:17).

Second we can rejoice because Jesus' going away to the Father was for our benefit – which gave way for the Holy Spirit to come and live within us. Just imagine the Spirit of the Father coming to live in us. Abba Daddy! No wonder we can rejoice - in the midst of sorrow, pain and grief we have Abba Father living on the inside of us to help when everything around us is being shaken.

Those who were fortunate to have a father around can attest to the fact that no matter how bad things got, daddy knew what to do. We experienced peace in the house in the middle of the storm. Daddy demonstrated his strength and we respected him. When daddy spoke, he released such authority that everything out of order got in order. We saw no need for fear.

Well, we have the Spirit of Truth – who is our Comforter and will show us the Father's will for this present age. We don't have to grope around in uncertainty as the world does. However, while we wait, we can be a beacon of light to a lost world. But if we can endure <u>just for a moment,</u> that moment will turn into perpetual joy for eternity.

Day 39

After the Dust Settles

1 Kings 19:13
And it was *so*, when Elijah heard *it*, that he wrapped his face in his mantle, and went out, and stood in the entering in of the cave. And, behold, *there came* a voice unto him, and said, What doest thou here, Elijah?

Elijah was used by God to call a people to decide who they would serve. He challenged Ahab (king of Judah) and his prophets to a duel. If God be God, let Him speak by fire – if your god be god, let him speak by whatever means! But choose whom you would to serve, and stop straddling the fence.

As the story continues, the Lord revealed Himself by fire which caused the people to admit that "The Lord, He is God" (1 Kings 18:39). Then Elijah instructed the people to siege the 450 prophets of Baal and kill them.

This does not make Ahab happy so he ran to Jezebel (his wife) to explain his depressed behavior; Jezebel, in-turn threatened Elijah's life.

<u>1 Kings 19:2</u>
Then Jezebel sent a messenger unto Elijah, saying, So let the gods do _to me,_ and more also, if I make not thy life as the life of one of them by to morrow about this time.

Verse three says – Elijah was afraid and he ran for his life!

<u>1 Kings 19:3</u>
And when he saw _that,_ he arose, and went for his life, and came to Beer-sheba, which _belongeth_ to Judah, and left his servant there.

The situations of life will threaten the very core of our being, especially when the wind starts to blow, the earth quakes, and then releases the tsunami all at the same time. We discover it is not unusual for something of this magnitude to hit us right after we do something great for God.

When this happens then we question if what we heard or did was from the Lord. Beware of the tactic of the enemy – to create doubt, confusion, and noise until we operate in unbelief. Unbelief happens when you are not sure initially – but doubt follows when you question what you initially believed, which is worse.

Elijah saw with his own eyes the great trials, the miraculous signs and wonders, the mighty hand and outstretched arm, with which the Lord had delivered His people. But the voice of Jezebel was so magnified that it had clouded his perception of the God who answered by fire. Therefore, Elijah ran and hid!

Even in our hiding, in a solitude place, after the dust settles, God will speak to us because there - we can hear His voice. It's the place where He reassures us of His love, help, and care – that we need not fear, but stay confident.

It is so apropos to end with these words, "For thus saith the Lord GOD, the Holy One of Israel; in returning and rest shall ye be saved; in quietness and in confidence shall be your strength..." (Isaiah 30:15).

Day 40

God Calls Us to Swim

Ezekiel 47:5
Afterward he measured a thousand; *and it was* a river that I could not pass over: for the waters were risen, waters to swim in, a river that could not be passed over.

We have been in the shallow parts of the water too long. God calls us to swim into the deep to catch bigger fish, to fulfill more needs, the place of greater works!

I believe the levels of waters (ankle, knee, waist and the deep) represent the mission fields Jesus speaks about in Acts 1:8, "But ye shall receive power, after that the Holy Ghost is come upon you: and ye shall be witnesses unto me both in Jerusalem, and in all Judaea, and in Samaria, and unto the uttermost part of the earth."

God calls us to go to the uttermost parts of the earth. We will find enough ground for us to cover. We all do not have to go to the same places as some regions of the world, our nation, state, city and our own neighborhood have not heard the word.

There rings a sound in my voice and words that I will articulate that only a certain nation will receive, and vise versa. The grain stands ripe for harvest; the choice is up to me to go!

I am not a swimmer. I took swimming lessons years ago and could not accomplish the swimming technique, due to my fear of drowning. I wanted so badly to learn but my fear of drowning out-weighed my desire to learn.

Therefore, I never ventured out of the shallow part of the water. As long as I could stand on <u>my own</u> and depend upon <u>my own strength</u> - I felt safe. My faith was washed out by my fear!

To accomplish what God is calling us to do, it is going to take faith to believe that we can do all things in Christ Jesus, who strengthens us (Philippians 4:13). Fear of the unknown and focusing on our inadequacies limits God to do the impossible. It is time to launch out into the deep. This is our hour because the current of the water flows at a steady pace moving in the right direction. DIVE IN!

About the Author

 Coraleen is a licensed evangelist of the gospel of Jesus Christ and has spiritual covering under Pastor Decker Tapscott, of Faith Christian Church, International Outreach Center in Warrenton, VA.

Coraleen has a prophetic anointing and has been called as a teacher for these end-times. She teaches Sunday school and discipleship class. She is known for her ability to instruct in a practical way.

Coraleen holds a B.S. in Business Administration, a Masters of Art in Christian Education where she was recognized as Valedictorian. She also holds a Doctorate of Ministry from Faith Christian University and Schools.

Coraleen has three daughters--Carmelita, Lakisha, Nichelle; a granddaughter, Racquel; and son-in-law, Malcolm.

Mailing address:
10723 Norman Ave.
Fairfax, Virginia 22030
703-934-4755
Email: Coraleen111@aol.com

Printed in the United States
147180LV00004B/6/A